NATURAL WONDERS

PREVIOUS BOOKS BY ANDREW SANT

Poetry
Lives
The Caught Sky
The Flower Industry
Brushing the Dark
Album of Domestic Exiles
Russian Ink
The Islanders
The Unmapped Page – Selected Poems
Tremors New & Selected Poems
Speed & Other Liberties
The Lives and Times of the Islanders
Fuel
The Bicycle Thief & Other Poems
Baffling Gravity
Near the Border New & Selected Poems

Essays
How to Proceed
The Hallelujah Shadow

Anthologies
First Rights – a Decade of Island Magazine
Toads

NATURAL WONDERS

ANDREW SANT

PUNCHER & WATTMANN

First published by Puncher & Wattmann in 2025
PO Box 278
Waratah NSW 2298

© Andrew Sant, 2025
© Cover photograph: Andrew Sant

The moral right of the author has been asserted.

ISBN 9781923099678

For Tina

CONTENTS

1

REDHEADS

Strike one
and it will flare

as Bryant & May,
an unlikely pair of thugs,

intended. It's a match
for anyone – branded

and named after the bright-
haired minority,

its stereotypes, hot-
headed, quick-

fisted, treacherous.
Judas Iscariot, in paintings,

looks scary. Does the Virgin Queen?
Van Gogh? Hopeful rumour

once had it, the genetic trait
would vanish, like a tribe,

but not, I can verify
calmly, in my family.

I am the conduit
for pheomelanin

and slurs, a combination
requiring the addition

of wit – tests, on junior
occasions, to rid the schoolyard

of a potential victim.
It's better to be a hit at lunchtime

than be punched. Sex, it's now said
in respected academic outlets,

is an even better proposition
when it's with a redhead

than with those of other
stunning hair colours, they must

require more rest – clever
whoever first made that brave

conjecture, it suggests
a need for further vital tests.

A CARTOGRAPHER DREAMS

In my dream the continents shift
   north and south, east and west, the uplifts
      from ocean bed to mountain range
are astonishing, a danger, as I focus,
   on shaky ground, my telescope.
      All this happens in a seismic moment. To get
the drift of this, think of supercontinents,
   Pangea, Gondwana, breaking up
      as easily as a lump of clay, the planet rumbling,
the consequences immense. It's so magnetic
   I need my compass. It's back to basics,
      after dark, with a sextant to fix
an angle on the North Star. It is bliss.
   There has not, for centuries, been any call
      for earthly calculations as big as this – not since
I dreamed of overhauling the medieval
   world map of Muhammad al-Idrisi
      on my study wall. I kept it free
of exonyms. I overslept. It seems
   I'm never far from work in bed –
      T-squares, dividers and protractors.
The work's my boss and, to be accurate,
   without it, awake or sleeping, I am lost.

TERRITORY

(Gymnorhina tibicen)

Magpies watch people
watching them – their sense
of separateness is shared.

Daily, there is a smart pair
on the grass, male
and female. They can hear things

we can't, such as the motion
of grubs underground.
They strut, pause

then strike, obedient
to gut hunger. Fly up, starkly
black and white, two

immaculately groomed
carollers on a telephone wire.
These calls clearly get through –

the park is theirs, entirely,
not counting other species
of bird (and people) toward

whom they are careless.
That's my assessment,
as an observer. At best I can

only guess where the magpies'
watched territory begins
and ends. It is possibly

somewhere near the border
where cross-species'
perception reaches its limits.

RELATIVE BEARINGS

So close to the boat, willows either side
brush it, their flexible branches
in fresh spring leaf
define an avenue of water.
Binoculars are of no use: no horizon.
The only birds, frightened,
are nearby coot. Since
quitting the ugly port
we've seen swans, egrets, tufted ducks.
Six passengers on the look out.
One of us, a man whose Teutonic name
I'll discover later, holds a large, new map.
Perhaps he knows exactly
where we are, turning the map
this way and that or,
more likely has not a clue
as if in a botched military manoeuvre.
Now there are flowering waterlilies,
bright yellow, beside the slowed boat
and, on sunlit pads, frogs,
big, brown and glistening
in the wider breadth of water.
They are authorities, no doubt,
on aquatic, positional matters –
and soon there are pelicans,
flying in formation overhead,
who could accurately track the boat,
one of three-hundred and twenty
remaining species of bird,
hereabouts, that daily get
watchers' definitive binoculars out.
Though not where the willows
are densest and close, which is mostly

when the water isn't wide and open
to the charter boat's speedier going.
The map the man's finger visits must show
a maze of channels, streamlets and lakes
for, evidently, it matters to him
where on his map of the Danube delta
we are by the minute
given how, within it, only a little
of the delta can be glimpsed –
about which the tall, resolute reeds
the boat skirmishes with merely hint.

THIS LOGGERHEAD TURTLE
at Mon Repos

How heavy she must feel
now that, out of the sea,
she's huge in the moonlight,
one of the planet's
great navigators, her flippers,
efficient in the deep, now
forcing her dark turtle bulk
up the beach, her heart
beating faster. The effort,
and her ancient reptilian head,
so like a fossil of itself,
wise-looking from its lone
submarine journeying,
solicit human tenderness.
Soon her clawed flippers
excavate a nest, fling back
the sand, last in a chain
of such preparations, here,
over decades. When she lays
her hundred or more eggs –
as if dripping from her
into the pit – she seems
in a daze or in bliss.
You, watching via binoculars,
see the genesis of risk,
the probability a single
hatchling at most will live
to tune into the appeal
of the earth's magnetic field,
and thereby return here,
the dome of its carapace
slowly emerging from the sea
lapping this beach some year.

REMOTE INTERSECTIONS

A raptor, way above the fences, sees
　　movement in short grass a mile away,
　　　　the somnolent town in the distance.

Soon, cruising on thermals, then circling
　　high over prey, the bird,
　　　　hawk or harrier, is a photorealist

of the skies, its binocular focus
　　on the subtle tones in rodent fur
　　　　and the fluorescence of scent trails.

A driver, when the road straightens
　　and intersections become an event,
　　　　sees a raptor, soaring, to his right or left

on the edge of his sight, a frequent
　　occurrence as he eliminates distance –
　　　　though thereabouts a fast car

being of any remote interest to that raptor
　　is monumentally doubtful, as it eyes,
　　　　with high resolution, a mouse.

SPIDER IN THE PUBLIC LIBRARY

Out there among the forests of books
    is a huntsman spider – this might be a million
years back or a million years hence
    for all it grasps of the time

required to borrow a novel.
    The spider, temporarily, is the hairy
long-legged denizen
    on a shelf of detective fiction,

though it would rather
    be under the habitual cover
of parched eucalyptus bark or,
    poised to flee, camouflaged,

and not cunningly spotted
    by a wild borrower,
an arachnophile, fresh
    from the natural history section

who comes to the rescue,
    which in the eight eyes of the spider
might be mistaken for a chapter
    on its imminent capture.

This species has outlasted alarm
    since before the break-up of Gondwana –
like a thief the big creature,
    on my open hand, freezes.

After going to treed safety, I vouch,
    as the borrower, the spider
will be coaxed to return to dry
    foliage, as if at the limit of a loan.

MISSION

A Nobel Prize
should be given for the exemplary
shining script
of the snail,

long after rain,
which, in its original way
across tricky terrain,
remains fearless.

WASPISH

If it wasn't for the sting
on the tip of my finger, I might not

have found their way in.
I shook the wasp off

and discovered its entrance
above the front door, an obscured crack

in the wall. I hid my acute pain.
But I wanted to settle the score.

How big was the hidden nest?
My finger bloomed red. Wasps

have a temper and a marvellous sense
of direction. Wild stripes.

They navigate by memorising
geographic features. When

I looked up, a number of wasps
were circling like planes

on hold over Heathrow –
the workers, most likely, not drones,

which can't sting. I prefer
those drones, though to tell

the difference it's necessary
to get close. I don't want

to be a pest, so keep
a suitable distance now

I've located their nest. Warn others.
Wasps have been victorious

killers since before Mount Everest
began gradually to soar,

are super insects, one of the best evolved
of all the menaces to us humans

at a picnic. Nevertheless, we're both
co-operative species

and broadly omnivorous,
and now, in this instance,

have in common, a house –
though about any assumption

neither of us need to move out
nor be massacred, I have doubts.

THE WATCHERS

Only the gullible or others
passing through who look down

would be taken in –
spotting from the swing bridge

a brown fur seal,
slumped upon rocks,

sun dry, ailing.
There he looks gravely

like one of the last
of his kind, eyes shut.

Whoever runs for help,
if help is to be found, returns

without it. Pity fills
the minutes. This seal's

repeated trick, before
his audience falls away,

is to suddenly roll
into the water, dive,

and always re-surface,
erect as a whiskered vicar

eyeing astonished mourners.

MAKING SNAKES

There are islands without snakes;
   it is a sin to bring them in.

      I am tempted to bet
         it's their agility on land

            without limbs that casts
              snakes as sinister

       to humans, plus their endless
     reptilian silence and tiny,

hard, unblinking eyes.
   We most value species – dolphins

       and chimps – that mirror, distantly, us.
      Snakes live near the edge

           of possibility, a creature
             so low-key it can live on its own

      all summer under a house
    before, when it's seen,

somebody screams. They
   are mostly extreme

       in length and in contrast
        to their width – a measure

           of their evolutionary success
          as a naturalist's eye

journeys slowly towards the tail
from a venomous head.

There is no better snake,
black or tiger, than the one

newly spotted – and if it's viewed
from a negative angle

that's because of attributes
we dare not handle.

METAPHYSICAL

Where there's not a whisker
of evidence, there's faith in the existence
of a preposterous, personal God,

yet when I spotted
the astonishing presence in our house
of a long-tailed, brown, hopping
marsupial mouse – soon caught
by my hand for swift release –

and then later recounted this,
there was universal doubt.

ABOUT THE SIZE OF MY PASSIONFRUIT VINE

The world seems an unlikely place,
a fluke in the universe,
until I contemplate, on a vine,
exemplary, spherical passionfruit.

*

I rashly propose, the sweet fruit,
in their bountiful number,
a sudden galaxy, sum up our wonder
at the cosmos, an incredible treat.

*

Don't pick the fruit, when ripe
it all drops; gravity will harvest it soon
whether you, the glad grower,
are ready or not. It is cosmic loot.

*

I planted the vine. Blind chance
is often evident, though not
in the fenced garden of mine.

Soon pilgrims, from all points
of the compass, arrive.

*

When, amazed, they enter
the garden, allowably
plunder it, in ones, twos

and often more, having heard
about the number of passionfruit
dangling and dropping,

I'm certain the pilgrimage, for some,
is partly driven by the deadly
sins of greed and blunt envy
not, in my friends, qualities I readily observe,
yet are remarkable when, shocked,
I suddenly spot them.
                 Nor, to make a point,
do I humbly hold back
from expressing some extreme
biblical wisdom, specifically,
the last shall be first – a threat made
to hasten restraint, hurled
at some of these worldly
feasters on sweetness.

*

Who would not be astonished! In particular,
now it's autumn, by how the fruit,
ripe with seed – revealed among
dense leaves – ball-shaped, turning oh so

slowly purple, looks, if not festive
then, in all sizes, bullishly testicular.

*

The tendrils sense, at a distance,
what to cling onto, garden wire for instance, extend
their thin green lengths, and coil around it.

With its starburst flowers, its gargantuan
growth, the vine shows no predictable limits.

*

I tell the pilgrims, in case they don't already know,
the fruit gets its name from the flower,
and the flower, in its parts, symbolizes
the Passion of Christ. Petals, anthers, stigma,

                                        oh yes,

it's a loose outdoor lecture, thanks, sadly,
to the first Spanish missionaries in the Americas.

It is called a clock flower in Greece,
a secular likeness. Some blessèd pilgrims (what
friends!) in their zealous quest for the crop, stress
there should be another time – and place –
for such supplementary, fruitless intelligence.

*

Within his welcoming Athenian garden,
Epicurus stated, in summary, 'Death means nothing to us.'
Thus, how much depends on luscious fruit.

*

Now I remember, I was a youth
when I first saw such a rampant exotic plant,
wild to a curious migrant
on the south side of the planet, freshly out
of a freezing European winter. The vine's clever

tendrils gripped my attention – the means
by which its lateral shoots got away in summer heat
from useful roots.

23

*

Before the vine, peas and runner beans
were the previous climbers –
poor yielders. Even worse in my garden

the awful nasturtiums, as an item
to eat. I pondered growing thirsty chayote.
Hit on *Passiflora edulis* during vigorous research.

*

Divide the smooth shell of the fruit
with a knife, scoop out
the seeds and the juice –
pips drip, in the yellow liquid, from lips,
all so sweet in the mouth
with a miraculous
hint of vitamin bitterness.
                              Or if down
on the ground, left late,
the shells soon wrinkled
and brittle on the way
to help germination, it's the sex
of breezy self-pollination, bee-free,
that has kept this purple species in seed –

a top recipe for earthly success
as is the juice loosed
upon vanilla ice cream;
the memory of it sure

to have almost melted away
when next year's crop, so
possibly prolific, starts to drop.

TWO SWIMMERS

Because it acknowledges
the tilted earth is turning
on its axis in space,
the first swim of the season
in the cold sea portends
less breathtaking immersions,
less baptismal, less bracing,
more consistent with the possibility
of a crowded beach later in spring
which, on this day, accommodates
several lone Pacific gulls,
snatching fingerlings in the shallows,
than people you can see
from way out in the water,
a few walkers, their dogs
putting oystercatchers to flight –
and then there's the other swimmer, far off,
now stroking back to the beach
who may also fancy she was born
to love wild water, albeit
briefly, her amphibian dreams
alive all winter in the city, the sea
now so wide and bright,
the waves – it's a clean ocean beach –
approaching the dunes in parallel action
while trained by the moon
and an offshore breeze,
perfect to tumble in or dive beneath,
all is motion and fluid
as it was in the beginning –
oh, the relief from being born to cleave
to the inducements of speech,
its meanness, mendacities

and – misemployed – mischief
when, with propelling kicks you go
deep underwater, and a last walker
on the beach sees his world has zoned
into a wide immaculate ocean …

PAREIDOLIC TRAVELS

After all, there are other people
    and other lands neither censuses
nor maps include, subject as ever
    to disputes – another world
where creatures gone extinct
    are resurrected in the sky, or the face
of a missing person reappears
    in a piece of toast – and where no cloud
of doubt troubles the Turin shroud.
    Is it better there without
a rolling news. Or actual gout?
    It's likely fevers or famine
favour multiple fleeting signs,
    and none of them concern
local roads; no knowing
    where branches of a tree may lead.
Elsewhere, someone's noticed
    a horrid outline in their porridge.
Strange to say, bright angels
    favour nightly windowpanes.
Every day there are more claims.
    Without taming it, the high hope
might be this glad shebang
    gets out of hand and visits slow –
till nimbostratus looks mainly
    like itself before sudden rains.

2

SEISMIC

You can visit Sicily
to witness Mount Etna signalling
with terrific white smoke, it's worth it,
but you'll find erupting
human behaviour at a busy *trattoria*
specific to Palermo, worth a pithy
sentence or two on Tripadvisor
or better, at length, a poem

which associates the business
with a seismic zone where trouble's
coming. The street is hectic, unaware.
The waiters, smartly dressed, are out there
touting pasta dishes, pizza, *pescare,*
all *autentico*, of the region.
Who, visiting, can resist?

Soon there are more patrons,
outside and in, than tables and chairs,
and still the soliciting
waiters on the street persist in pressing
their lucrative, authentic dishes
blind to what's impending, out the back,
in the depths of the mean kitchen.

Never go by appearances
in a seismic zone – or any – the polite
welcome, the steady poses. You,
off for a piss, near the kitchen, have glimpsed
what's over-cooking with the chefs.

Steam there or – startling! – is it smoke?
Wild faces above stoves, bright red as lava.

Grimy aprons. Little room to move and hurry
meal after meal after violent meal
but enough space for an abrupt
and rapid flow of local expletives
which, aptly, utter looming trouble.

A SHORT HISTORY OF CIVILITY

The enmity of two men entering
a famous city gate at dusk
was wrecked when they heard
of a common enemy's murder
and slapped one another on the back.

This act was witnessed five thousand
years ago, a wise woman's word.

Thus spread, in that dry territory –
now an archeological site –
the practice of cordial greeting
on the street, and those friendly
waves of the arm which had the added
attraction of banishing flies.

For the people could see it was good,
a civil lubricant – not
lost in translation, or buried
during subsequent millennia
in spite of the tribal bloodshed
and the rubble.
                         Civility was often,
in the settlements, all that was left.

So now whenever, on the street,
a casual salutation is traded, brightly,
eye to eye, it is agreed by many,
though not stated, the width
of a free smile beats that of a knife.

HOSTILITY LESSONS

The small boy won't remember
throwing stones, one after another,
he loses count, at the family of magpies
on the grass, seized
by the power and pleasure of it,
the birds moving judiciously away
from the missiles but not
exhibiting fright, while
the boy's well-dressed mother looks on

at her smart little man, doing,
she possibly reckons, what is natural
and most certainly doing naught to combat
such inane, thuggish hostility.

What do you do, lecture
the woman? Show her a man's modest fist?
(She's showing off her number one tyrant.)
Then let her hurl twenty rocks of invective fairly
in your direction? The male magpie,
now the birds' nesting is over,
is not aggressively swooping
on these two roaming strangers.

The boy won't remember,
in a week, a month, a year in the suburb,
what comes as easily to his species,
since before the Neolithic,
as picking up countless sticks.

He may be lost thereafter in the future –
and if his mother (though it could
now be his father) still has anything to say
about him to the neighbourhood,
it's that nothing – watch out! –
had better get in his way.

LAURA BRANIGAN IS DEAD

Those opening chords again, penetrating the racket
    of a café – heard last time, possibly,
in a supermarket or a bar.

An American hit, a worldwide smash,
    now playing in Romania, during lunch. *Gloria.*
More than thirty years since it was recorded.

Gloria is 'always on the run'
    in that memorable, uptempo, desolate song
that is nearby however far from home

you are and, presumably, the singer
    is still getting royalties from it.
Sad to relate, I soon discover,

the money must flow to her estate.
    Vividly, I can remember her persuasive hips
as on TV she performed her hit,

her raven hair and striking face an illustration
    for her Irish name. And thus recalled her
during lunch in that bad café.

Then wondered how she is going now,
    as we casually say, since nothing I'd overheard
or read offered any direction. Instead,

wi-fi connected, the new old news:
    Laura Branigan is dead. The song, her afterlife.
Outside that café, a harder matter to digest.

TRACTION

Obedience to traffic lights
will never catch on,
a future memoirist reckoned
in 1920, Paris, watching drivers ignore them.
Others, terrified of the industrial speed
of early trains, thought the same.
My truculent uncle was the young observer
visiting France.
                    I once thought
the possible future ubiquity
of mobile phones was all talk.

A fellow Homo sapiens, among the first
to plough the land somewhere
in Mesopotamia, found
scorn stuck to him like dust
on a successful hunter.

Copernicus was, at first, not to be trusted.
The Sun is a convenience for the Earth
which, many vocal Americans know,
was formed by God a few thousand years ago.

When a good idea gains traction
(perhaps originally of a car or train)
many folks often get left behind,
a leading authority claims.

Mobile phones, one day, will be replaced
by advanced telepathy, I claim,
every time I lose mine. Try it –

before Capitalism, a juggernaut,
finally collides – some folks left behind –
with countless attractive atoms on the planet
when fresh brakes cannot be applied.

STRANGE BLINDNESS

Suddenly, a man is running
as if he has heard a starting gun.
Out of a park, he sprints towards the street;
looks fit, forties, and is dressed in black.
There are two small children, girls,
also running, into the distance
along the pavement. Perhaps
they are his fleeing kids. But no,
alarmingly, as he runs past them,
he acknowledges them not at all.
It is a long, quiet street, a stranger
to the police. The man, without stopping,
tears off his jacket. Either he is hot
or planning on a marathon;
whatever strife awaits, or doesn't,
he's not now running for his life
to get about with more
endorphins – he's not a jogger –
and besides, he's surely heading
for a specific place. You, transfixed,
on an overlooking balcony,
cannot take your eyes off him –
and think it's an error to carry, always,
a mobile phone; who knows
what mad news might be brewing.
Luckily, it seems, the running man
has stamina, although however
much he might wish, it won't
allow him to shake off his
panic, like a virus, catching.
Now, he has reached a far-off
crossroads and, without
a backward glance to get

the measure of his acceleration,
swerves to the left, hard, an edge,
his breath the one imperative, as if,
when no-one else can yet agree
to see it, he's running from
a tsunami or a crumbling cliff.

THE LANGUAGE TEACHER

The teacher never spoke to me,
with personal warmth, in French.
Aimer, for instance, he taught
his class of boys to conjugate
in unified high, unbroken voices.
What he wanted to pursue after school
was also a regular advancement
of instruction. He, cleverly,
singled out a student, an only child
with an unmodified English accent.
I was, briefly, top of his antipodean class.
The teacher knew exactly want he wanted.
This he made clear, in his new car,
when he, agreeably, drove me back
to a cold home that lacked a vigilant mother.
He taught me, with authority, what he
desired in the language of his hands.
I had his complete attention
over days, weeks, months,
though the psychosexual term
for what he liked I wouldn't learn
till long after he had abruptly flown
with his wife, lately our housekeeper,
who I'd now name as his enabler.
Soon, I could pass an examination
on the necessary skills of a handsome
man of his persuasion, yet he knew
I didn't then have the language,
opportunity, or need to blab
to create an engrossing exposé –
no such need in Ancient Greece –
and can't see one happening now,
but could for fun be tempted here,

belatedly, to make his name
into a mad anagram – make it
the title! – as a bored pupil might,
waiting impatiently for the school bell.

THE DEATH OF RECORD DAVE

Thousands of vinyl records,
pop, blues, rock and jazz,
he placed in alphabetical order
in his upstairs St Kilda flat,
well-kept companions for a man
who liked a social drink, a chat
about rare pressings that he owned,
whose diffidence made it hard
to get to know him beyond
his nickname and reputation.
He came and went from pubs
and parties with the best backing
of the bands, his LPs, expertise, decades
in the making, like strata, ageing,
presumably, in every room.
Few had seen them. He wasn't daft.
He was at home like a glad librarian
who'd swiftly placed an early
closing sign – a precious groove
requires unusual concentration.
The note he left, for the record,
to whoever it may concern, reputedly
said it was time for him to go
while he was still content. Then
he clicked the door. With him
that afternoon, not one needy song,
among the thousands, pleaded.

RIDICULOUS

1

A lone white duck on grass
beside a highway is a rare thing
to come across, out of place,
in danger. It has escaped.

Each time I approach, the duck
waddles off to what it considers
is safety near another tree. The speed
of the traffic reflects a need

for people to be elsewhere quickly
on a thoroughfare not fit
for a duck to roam across.
Slowly, I again approach it,

the stupid bird, which does not get
that I'm its saviour. If it could fly
the distance between us
would soon be fine, now it's ridiculous.

2

This is when I inform the police.
I say, 'There's an imperiled
domestic duck beside the highway
that might cause a traffic pile up.'

I reason, if the cops can catch
an unlucky crook, they will be
a match for a wayward duck.
The person in uniform looks at me

with forensic interest, saying little,
from which, at length, I gather means
the equivalence I'd seized upon
via my reasoning is simply wrong.

The police could not give a fuck
about someone's wonderful lost
white duck beside a frantic highway.
My words. The cops found no more to say.

MEDITERRANEAN SOLO

The songbird, overheard,
    is not on a branch
of its own choosing
    or anywhere near one,
yet it sings from daybreak to dusk,
as if a storm has cleared
    and now the sun is appearing.
There are no trees nearby
    nor is the bird to be seen –
a finch most commonly,
    often a migratory species,
nifty and quick in flight,
    among small flocks. Its song
as surely encourages
    such a reflection as would
its skittish swiftness trick the talons
    of a plummeting raptor.
Then it would live
    to sing over and over again,
high-pitched, thrilling –
    the bird possibly both
heard *and* seen, free,
    close to the Mediterranean sea.
It's the open curtains and window
    observed from a street below
that promote the solo;
    and the show – as long
as the resident owner
    is home each night to close them –
must go, daily, on and on.

KANELO

Pack animals, reverting
to the wild, the street dogs of Greece
will follow your fear, at a distance,
along a deserted street,
angling to attack.

But one young dog,
cinnamon-coloured –
so he is called Kanelo –
was alone, a reject,
wary, shy, needy
like a child in a playground
who needed to be included.

Our protection in exchange
for his safety. A bargain!

Poor little dog, his penis,
pink as lipstick, stuck firmly out
of its sheath – he needed a vet –
kept his carnivore hungers
in check till, in some shadowy spot,
we left him nourishment.

He was, ever at a distance,
the facsimile of someone's pet.

Until trust eventually won.
It was his stomach, after three years,
that commanded it, and then the shelter
he no longer lacked. Only yesterday

for the first time –
accepting human affection –
he rolled onto his back.

MEDICAL DEVELOPMENTS

In the Hospital Clinic Waiting Room

Having taken my place
as a seasoned patient
at the umpteenth appointment
in numerous bare, functional
medical rooms, I surveyed,
in the way a CAT scan cannot,
the individual demeanours –
the resigned outnumbering the resolute –
of those on the blue, institutional seats,
I now sat with, some probably
also survivors of a recent
surgical intervention masked only
by their dignified composures,
no-one any longer compelled
to wear a white-gown
on this shared occasion
of generalised tedium, a tribute
to the wish to move off soon
into the world of the well. Thus
continuously occupied
with the immediate prospects,
interrupted by the rare departure
of one of us down a long
foreboding corridor, I spotted
at the end of a row, on the floor,
a solitary earthenware pot
and in arid soil there's no longer
a conspicuous plant,
as once surely there was,
whose endurance must
have succumbed to the recurrent

mood of the room, but instead
two small shoots, weeds
mysteriously thriving
which showed, upon my very
close examination, sizeable hope.

The Numbers

Probability usefully suggests
it won't, of course, happen
to you but, as surely, to others.

A friend's diagnosis is also a chance
to exhibit disbelief
as if she'd been gunned down

on the street, and certainly
the prognosis is a specific clue
to a final how and when

in view of the grave
genetic variant that's come
into the family, a barely believable –

the maths done – random first one:
a delinquent cell that now rouses
treatment, a budding killer,

a fucking tough little number.

The Man on File

Since the suspicion, the raised alarm,
days chilling into a wintry narrative,

I've kept a file on myself –
as if I've assumed a self-disguise,

a dark identity – to keep an eye
on my movements. There's correspondence

for medical appointments, scans,
results of tests. I'm a man on the road

to a big operation, date set, the build up
drumming through the months as it might

for a spectacular daylight heist.
It's like, at my age, a new occupation.

It's criminal, I seem symptom free.
Rely on, to be sure it's not a con, those

with letters trailing their shiny names
and eye-raising fees, to explain, to confirm

the proposed action is not out
of proportion to the perceived situation –

as blind sceptics reckon about the science
biting those of us frightened by global climate change …

These cold days, extensive, there's a guy
on file I'm forever trying to recognize.

Terms

Tell me it's medical name, I said,
referring to a post-surgery issue,
so I can research it. Too rare, unlike
a tumour, to yet take my blame for days
in a hospital bed, the specialist team,
standing in attentive condescension, told me.

These weeks I am unexpectedly expanding
my medical lexicon. Test me tomorrow,
you who'll be grouped to look down
on me as I look up from my laptop computer,
be grateful for what you'll find next:
prime evidence for a refereed text.

Blood

The nurses, the cleaners,
the orderlies, anaesthetists, doctors,
surgeons and who knows who else at work
in the hospital, with a uniform
purpose, number among them
hundreds who by birth
are Sri Lankan, Vietnamese or Turks.

My blood is taken by a nurse
who speaks native Cantonese – the sample
to find what type gives me life. I am pale
from an internal bleed, found
once the question of why
excuses me of my normal complexion.

She can see my right arm
is already bruised black and blue.

I say, to crudely amuse us,
I am a person of colour.

My blood group, I later discover
is, among the world's population,
the most compatible, common.
It's a litre I need. I'll want someone
out there to thank. Maybe,
to start with, all of humanity. I want
a congruent transfusion –

all the more for the small assurances
of the El Salvadorian nurse
who gives it, a *mestizo*
whose family, she tells me, fled
civil war, got away to the border,
through summer heat and flooded
coffee plantations, where others lost blood.

Neighbours

They speak too loudly, watch TV
with the sound up, programs
I've never heard of. Also soaps.
One has a birthday that's close.
What I know about their vocal
relatives, who visit, steadily grows.
Many are from Albury/Wodonga,
four long hours by train. Words
I've overheard from nurses
about their ailing cousin might
exercise them, though
not the fact that he's a snorer
who surely lets it be known
he's at home even when doors

and windows aren't open.
My neighbours are never alone
without their phones. The curtains,
semi-circular, attempt by design
to confine privacy. None of us might
recognise each other, by choice,
off the ward though I'd know
at any distance their voices. .
Maybe they've kindly thought
there might yet be more
to me, some talk, while, curtained,
I freely read myself to sleep,
holiday fiction – that lovely last resort.

Declaration
war poem

Rock stars, sportsmen and actors
are fighting a battle, forcibly
enlisted into the language of conflict.

The news of a celebrity's lasting good
health has little attraction.
Someone must headline a broadcast.

It had better be one of them, overtly public,
when their lives are in danger.
Until 'After a long battle …'

and 'She lost her fight with …'
is aired, the metaphors, exhausted,
can't get any rest or hostilities cease.

Medical Developments

The stainless-steel instruments, as shiny
as they are sharp, of many sizes

and potential varieties of torture
seemed, one hopes, less awful after local sick

or injured colonials breathed in chloroform.
The instruments are on display in a cabinet of surgical

and other historical objects. I've been a cautious
patient in the hospital where they can

be pondered, near the conference room door,
down a long corridor. Louis Pasteur

was soon to expound germ theory
when the hospital was founded. Back then,

it took months fraught with nautical
terrors to sail this far from France.

One of the instruments on view reminded me
of a *petite* guillotine. I hope it was fast.

Mementos
  earplugs

The only way to restore them
to full but feeble employment,
their glory, is in the present tense –

the man in the next bed is snoring;
snored yesterday, will do so again.
High decibels, small ward.

I wear earplugs – might find
they're still in force sometime after
I've left, far from being deaf.

The Man in the Lift
  for Tina

It wasn't the fact that his wife
has a brain tumour that soon mattered most,
though the background geography
retained its importance – their farm
in up country Victoria, cattle, some dabbling
in grapes; their weekly stall
in the nearby town market was significant

otherwise, we later agreed, he wouldn't have mentioned it
to you that afternoon in the hospital lift
and then, on your daily visit,
you told it all to me. As well as his need
to stay in a hotel nearby
to be close to his wife

who, I could see
was, like me, fortunate,

cared for, loved, by the one necessary visitor
at the bedside, a chair next to it
no longer spare. What then

mattered most was the man
taking, by chance, the same lift up
with you again, days later,
and then you, seated, telling me the news
from him is now good –
and I thought how one day all
that might matter to us, for the hell of it,
for the shared relief, will be a long drive north
to a town, its weekly market, their stall.

THE WHISTLER

Though he cannot now be seen
he can be heard, whistling
a melody,
        the top notes
reaching at least the crown of a tree.

On the street, my side of the fence,
and a sometime whistler myself,
I'm stalled by his impressively liquid gift.

It shows there's no longer agony nor anguish,
no fair pleasure set to be legally attacked,
no-one coming to repossess
the furniture and house – the radio-exposed armies
have as good as abandoned their weapons,
and no-one, in the once smoking villages,
will be raped;
        and the reverberations
of the road drilling machine, days of them now
– which may have reminded the whistler
of a Dr Hammer DMSc, his reclining
chair and dental apparatus – have ceased.

Let whistling, its visitation
independent of age and gender,
be a spontaneous presence
street by street, no obligation,
in this neighbourhood – let its spirit go forth,
as do birds across patrolled borders,
in the knowledge that its melodies
are always unfettered, free

and perhaps released somewhere
one amazingly peaceful afternoon
to an audience of leaves.

Let no whistler think to be envious
of a superior whistler!

THE BICYCLE AND ITS RIDER

I need a new lock, need a new light,
   I'm taking my bike out of retirement.
It's been inert in the shed, the shed's a dump,
   the tyres haven't swallowed air
since I lent, like money, my pump
     to someone who didn't return it –
now I'm in a bicycle shop to buy a new one.
   The shop is crowded with bikes
at the start of their lives. I admire them.
   Perhaps I wouldn't if mine was nearby.
It's still, in retirement, taking time
    to speed free of it with my loyal help,
its revival delayed. I don't regret
    going away, limping in Italy, then in Spain –
in places remote as subconscious drives.
   I didn't miss riding, after I fell.
Neither carbon dioxide nor many
   motorists respond to a bicycle bell.
 I'll need a new one of those as well.
   Here this shop's the first stop
on the long road to an exit, non-toxic,
   from the untimely retreat
of both a bike and its rider – none other
   than me, a speed lover, recovered.
I'd rather die on the hard saddle,
   despite its damage, than manage
this mortal coil in a limousine
   briskly driven. I'm after lubricant oil.
And new brakes. So many parts needed.
   Everywhere, so many hazards.
Where must it all end? There'll be nothing
   to fret about after the hidden last bend.

DETERMINATION

is like stairs
or steps that never stop
going up and going down,
same place and time,
ruthless and paradoxical,
fast or slow (you'd
never know), though
that's no reason not to call
all stairs flights and, necessarily,
why people fall down them,
which escalates if they're severe,
a great expense of breath, hence
the invention of musty lifts,
which declare, for the fit,
a weakness notwithstanding
gigantic buildings, yet will never
get the better, in Rome's
torpid air, of the splendid
Spanish Steps, they never
cease to please,
they are determined –
as were their architects –
and, like others lesser known,
exceed themselves
continuously, are seen,
like all the active stairs
in homes, to paralyse defeat …

3

AMERICAN WONDERS

The pointed conifers looked stark
   on that clear night, against a full moon –
in their shadow, my tent, small
   in vast Yellowstone National Park.
I could hear wolves, wildly attuned
   to that lunar phase, far away
in the mountains. Eerie but I wasn't
   fearful, sitting on a log, sipping whisky.
It was the geysers, the petrified
   forest, the hot ponds, I'd come to see,
but chiefly Columbia spotted frogs. Now
   I'd added them to my growing list
of sightings, uniquely those
   of a lone herpetologist. The frogs
are not easy to spot. Thank god
   for my galoshes. There seemed
so few people about I could hike
   wherever I liked and freely get lost. Then
find my way back to a track
   shown on the map, which led me
to the place where I dumped
   my pack. Heavy but I was thrillingly
fit for my mission and still had supplies.
   I lit a small fire, added stream
water to a dried Thai curry. It tasted
   home cooked. The aroma must have lingered.
The astringent whisky cleared
   my nostrils, like roads. When the moonlight
suddenly exposed, between the trunks
   of gloomy conifers, a fellow biped,
huge, and soon approaching –
   likely attracted by the food – I dared
not, at first, reckon on its height

and girth to be the outline of a bear.
Specifically, a grizzly. It grunted.
    If I were a hunter I might have gone
for my gun. But I simply wondered
        at its presence. Then, passed by me,
it dumped its full weight, gently,
        like a massive sack off the back
of a truck, onto my tent. To show
        that I'd already had enough,
I sat my ground, called its bluff.
    The bear fancied my last supplies. Kind
of him to try to ignore me, a strong guy
        with a soft spot for frogs, who gets lost,
is easily slighted. So I soon tossed
        him westwards via a vigorous headlock.
His fur smelled like old socks. It was worth
        witnessing his shock, among the conifers,
as if this all was fiction. Under the stars
        he seemed to me like the double
of some dark personal trouble, overcome.
    The bear had given up, seemed –
on all fours, gradually retreating –
        not to be in peak shape, while I took deep
necessary breaths, unsteady on my feet.

BULLISH

How could anyone forget
that famous jersey bull kept
apart from the herd, the harsh bellow,
his steam breath in winter,
a padlocked slide bolt
imprisoning him in his pen,
and in summer the potent smell
of bovine confinement,
the packed mass of muscular
threat from shoulders
to haunches, while he moodily
stamped a front hoof.

He eyed children, slyly.
He could, on the loose, toss
one of us skywards.
His running, in the open,
was a terrible thunder.
His mouth loosed skeins of saliva.

Out in the everlasting English fields
he'd mount cows on heat, drive
his pizzle in, earn his hard
living and his relief.
                              Yes,
I remember him,
now that his image
has long been confined in my head –

within generous proximity
of those palaeolithic bovine
paintings in the Lascaux Caves
and not far from the charging
bronze bull seen near Wall Street.

APPETITE FOR FLIGHT

A bird that cannot fly
appeals to our own
forms of distress –

the young blue-winged parrot,
waterlogged in grass
after a deluge

could not be spurred to rise
by me or fear, so,
in its panic, I took it home

in the hope it might
recuperate in safety.
It may have been too late

for the bird to have any
prospect of rejoining
its small flock,

often found
nearby, on the ground,
feeding on seeds.

Relief is the reward
if human meddling
can save a wild creature.

The exhausted parrot,
banished from the authority
of the clock, rested

in a lightless box,
compulsory night, eyes,
I supposed, closed,

its bright plumage –
red, yellow, green, blue –
off duty. Might it die?

Sooner or later,
a scrabbling sound
replied when presumably

the bird was dry,
had fed on the seeds
I'd provided.

The sky had cleared.
The box was now a prison
on the ground, whose flaps

I opened – no predators
around ¬ and light
crashed in upon

the frightened parrot
that lost its balance, staggered
into the green freedom,

then battled gravity
while trapped by a baffling
lack of nerve, it tried

and tried to overcome.
Until, across millennia, all
of the relayed brilliance

of the species sought
its purpose in this bird
and found it, at first

in low uncertain flight
above the grass, like a learner –
I, watching, am in its class –

till learning more, the bird newly
prized its core appetite near
trees, and then it soared.

MANY SEA URCHINS

No wonder sea urchins have survived
other species wipeouts –

safe in rocky crevices
they are a menacing sight

for exterior defence.
All those threatening spikes!

Voracious feeding on algae
occupies their lives.

Only resident fools
would plunder their predators

and let numbers boom –
then soon a marine

plague's on the move.
Nevertheless, their gonads,

as any gourmet will agree,
are delicious, smooth

on the tongue, salty and sweet.
I have a flint fossil of one

perfect specimen urchin,
transported in chalk cliffs

from the Cretaceous –
so well preserved it serves

an aesthetic purpose.
This was worth recollecting

after, in rocky shallows,
I'd carelessly put my bare foot

on a contemporary version.
The lasting pain from its venomous

spikes is for the brave.
It was at the sad end of a lovely

exotic summer from which
I couldn't walk away.

THE YANGTZE

Never to return
to the longest river
in Asia, travel for days
along a stretch of its narrowing
then widening length –
many years since
I set out from an old wharf
in restive Chongqing, a hazard
to locate the modest boat, time
running out. Time, doubtless
won't allow a repeat
journey, should I desire it,
time at a premium
or squandered and, knowing this,
now, I recall, where we'd
moored on the riverbank,
being in the streets
before the waters rose
and drowned Fengdu.
In my hand a bag of sweet lychees
I'd bought from an old man's stall –
one of memory's trick
insinuations. The crew
on the boat spoke no English,
their passengers, except one,
were all Taiwanese. We might,
but for a few words,
have been signalling
to each other under water,
were there visibility. Meantime,
we pointed to the bold markers,
high up in the valley,
that showed the mad

height to which the waters would rise
for Mao's emphatic dream dam.
For the time being
the finless porpoise was not
yet extinct; nor, for now,
the Chinese alligator,
river turtle or salamander,
sick from swimming
in industrial and human shit,
visible from the boat where
not one of us who could afford
to board it would have failed
to act on symptoms
of personal ailment –
the vessel making long progress
where peasants throughout the dynasties
swam in clear depths of the river,
free of traveller comparisons.
A current prognosis: bad
from siltation and erosion havoc.
Time fled in the twentieth century
with man-made speed
and its wreckage – the waters
of the Yangtze, early in the blazing
new millennium, set to escalate
the rate. No time, therefore,
to delay making for the wild
Three Gorges, the boat,
from which we all gawped
upwards, small in their shadows,
a lesson in perspective, precious
as a site birds of passage
need for survival. The sheer
limestone sides a backdrop
for the Taiwanese with their cameras
poised for each one

and only frozen moment.
She was like a rare bird
or a celebrity among them,
a beautiful distraction, lit
by her own energy, a focus;
as the beam of her smile
increased, the Gorges receded,
the smile an enticement for,
possibly, all of Taipei.
Hard for them to see past
the woman's laughter,
she was bright health
sponsored by wealth, and
for her companions
an illumination. In the dark,
sleepless, my cabin light off,
blind to the river, I saw
as if from a sidewalk
the consequent enthralments
of power and greed, their glamour,
primed by the brightly lit cliffs
of a city, time's digits,
and, more clearly now,
squandered energy, its limits –
then, with daylight, viewed
the heedless wide river,
earth-coloured, churning,
that would rise in time,
at its world's end, to supply it.
At Yichang, that massive
generating dam, a pale
precipice, with its capacity
to influence the rotation of the planet
and amplify collective hubris.

NEXT WORKS
for Jan Senbergs

The thing to do is to keep on going,
the artist, pleased among his paintings, said –
three more years of work, a wild wind blowing.

All in his mind a wild wind blowing
around his lived-in body, his elemental head,
white haired because he has kept on going.

Big canvases are where he keeps on going
with oils for his capricious landscapes, instead
of tackling harsh terrain, real winds blowing.

He used to do so. His windy world is blowing
up, he sniffs the apocalypse in his paint, dead
certain that he still must keep on going.

Once he was spritely. Now he keeps on going
toward his next exhibition. Time has sped.
It's a brisk cliché to say winds of change are blowing.

Grotesque machines, he's shown, have spread
in all directions, like wreckage and common dread.
When great winds of any sort are blowing
the only thing to do is to keep on going.

UMBRELLA

Dormant, dangling and pampered,
it's best positioned to survive
another season, dry,

while, outside,
light in the street ebbs
under a threatening sky.

Opened under a wild
deluge, the poor thing is tested –

less wind and it's far
less tricky to have marvellous sex
underneath it

in a public park, mid-summer,

than for one of the coy lovers
to go home alone hoping
to keep under cover without courting
a soaking –
           the ill-adapted
thin spokes ever reacting
to imaginary tornadoes.

                  Now,
from a high window
there are suddenly water-
lily pads below; yes, they
really look in the city
to be so, dark lily pads
supported by spokes

and beneath them a crowd
with inherited Devonian
amphibious inklings – dependably

primed to soon get everyone home
with renewed aquatic pleasure
under buggered umbrellas.

GASTROPOCENE

A single snail
that I avoid stepping on in the rain
reminds me of a former plague.

One garden gastropod, or a few,
are good to observe

as they glide by on their mucus,
their eyes on the end of fine tentacles
searching, presumably,

for more food, my lettuces.
All they want is their share.
Each one is a primal, mobile stomach.
It's early summer,

so they're well out
of hibernation, shell-safe, and there are eggs
to be laid following their marathon
hermaphroditic sex in the sun
during spring.

They are welcome to a crisp leaf
or two, after all we are fired
by desires in common, but they are not, in my view,
free to covet a whole crop.

After a few months away
I returned to see how major
a modest absence can be.

The brown snails had overrun
path, courtyard, walls, at first anything freshly green
and now, desperate, a plague, were devouring
bark on the young lemon tree.

What had happened to their ready predators?
It was, to my possessive eyes,
like a vision of catastrophe,

an invasive population out of whack,
a crashed habitat,
with possible human parallels,
and soon, faced by my tough
intervention with a bucket
to remove them, a prelude to their doom.

DEGREES OF SCENERY
65º N, 19º W

Coming upon a fjord,
suddenly, looking far down
then out to sea, a deep blue beneath
a bright sky, the new viewers
will most likely angle
their cameras to capture
not the texture of sheer
basalt cliffs, but from a point
of prized orientation, the vista.
Earlier, there was a volcano to see,
smoking idly, as if on holiday.
Nothing yet grows in the last
outpouring of magma, now in paralysis,
though it inspires visions
of fire where gentle snow
still falls, as it should,
at this latitude in early spring.
Fire and ice (yesterday's lakes
were deep frozen); complementary
extremes to, by hire car,
purifyingly choose between.
From a distance, at sunset,
a mountain ridge, out of the clouds,
is jagged like an erratic
seismogram. The sun
unmists the sloping, grassy
farmlands, exposed by snowmelt,
between where glaciers retreat,
slowly yet inexorably,
and black sand grows the beaches.
Then, with a hard degree
of visibility, to look ahead
through the windscreen,

is to miss, along a highway,
on one side the advertised
white-capped mountain heights,
on the other, way below,
another vital test for vertigo –
and, regarding both, another
opportune photo, lost, of a scenic view
on an icecold day, since
there is, always, a surfeit.
Each work on the eye,
exclusively, where people
cannot abide. What, for basic use,
can be produced anywhere
near a névé field or high scree?
Viewed from afar both are,
paradoxically, scenic yet wild.
Or later there's a geyser,
a hot thermal spectacle, to see.
By now, a few hostels on,
the car and it's keen passengers
(spoilt aliens with a GPS)
are quick to drive further across
a seemingly vast, newly hatched planet –
to enter, at last, a fishing village
with its picturesque steeple
and, perhaps, token police who,
for want of any serious crime,
might stop a foreign driver
speeding past more, then
yet more, scenery – or else quiz,
reluctantly, reckless villagers
who, to a degree, are over it.

NOSTALGIA

Rain and more rain,
pinstripe, plashy or pittering rain
gaining, daily, its reputation
for variations on a theme; applause
on the iron roof a constant
and rather uncool.
                                    Nostalgic,
I play 'Rain on the Roof'
by the Lovin' Spoonful.
                                    The rain
roars.
        If I could find and play 'Rain'
by the Beatles, no doubt stoned
when they sang it, there'd surely
be more of the same: the weather
has a taste for nostalgia,
the sixties.
                    Pretty freaky!

Bob Dylan. 'Rainy Day Women'. Maybe.
Man, anything from that indisputably wet
decade and its freewheeling
idioms.
                The revolutionary mood
floods indoors, ever so
lachrymose, soothed by gloomy day blues.

Nostalgia is longing, dammed,
diverted back.
                No hassle;
I'm soon soaked on a bridge, glad

to look down
on a creek thunderously
overpower its staid, bushy banks –

urban detritus, like passé idioms,
getting snagged
or washed away,
                        about which
            some suitably firm words
would not go astray ...

THE TEMPORARY THIEF

Deep shadows on a moonlit evening,
   and hardly distinct from them
      two figures moving around a house
      they know is vacant overnight.
The man is nervous, his wife
   is soon inside with the crowbar
      she's used to wrench the sash
      window open. Let's leave her
to case the joint, oblivious
   to what's happening outside
      since this faux burglary is easy
      work. Her spouse, on watch
for threats or neighbours,
   in the cold garden, is soon sure
      he's being followed by eyes
      that, unlike his, are not compromised
by the dark. He's never been so
   preternaturally observant until now
      or in the past aided any thief,
      though he's always thought
his wife reads too much tough
   crime fiction, like off-duty police.
      It's an owl's wide eyes
      surveying the subdivisions,
and him, from a nearby chimney,
   that first makes him uneasy – though
      he's not sure of the species –
      and horridly exposed. He fears
that if it screeched he might suddenly
   join his wife. She too, he thinks,
      is so often a nocturnal wonder.
      Then it's the searching eyes
of a rodent, quickly skirting

around his feet, that prompts him
        to want to run. He is watched.
                Soon by a ringtail possum, feeding
in a camellia, no, it's at least two.
        Oh, how the eyes on him now multiply.
        He moves about. What a surprise
                to find, or be found out by, so
much wild nocturnal life! Inside
        there may be geckos eyeing
                his young wife whose mission –
                to dabble in crime so she
can realistically fictionalise it –
        he hopes soon will be over.
                Now past midnight, unless
                he's dreaming, it's not her
who is enduring, as if in a gothic
        horror movie, huge spooky
                bats flying low overhead. But
                it's certainly him, a compliant man,
trying to ignore tense movement
        in dense shrubbery (or is it
                his clandestine vision) and pairs
                of sinister, unblinking eyes.
Those cats watch him, and later
        see his empty-handed wife
                at last climb back outside –
                then slowly lower the window
on her fearless, interior chapter.

DEEP DAYS OF A DENDROCHRONOLOGIST

A tree, in a big wind, sways
  in its accumulated annual rings,
    and I imagine cross-sections. A stone

lobbed into a deep pond reveals
  a likeness in the concentric circles
    of the ripples – time enough, watching them,

to slowly say *dendrochronology*
  twice, and spell it, to someone
    puzzled by my quiet occupation. Of the past

the rings of a tree are silent, an unopened book,
  until I'm exposed to their tight chronology,
    and then, interpreted, they speak.

I've often found which year the earth
  circled the sun and governed the weather
    of my birth, within the girth of an oak.

Time circles out from a centre
  and all there is to foster equilibrium
    is daily existence on the far rim.

The year of my death
  will be a completed circle, a weather
    record, when I fall, perhaps

on ice, or under the sun, having run
  out of time to read a tree, growing,
    all my life, as much as a metre thick

though a mere fraction of a well kept
    slice of slow-growing, ancient
        huon pine, kauri or sequoia.

If I run my loving forefinger
    from the centre to the edge of a recklessly
        chain-sawed trunk, I may be tracing

evidence of more than two thousand summers,
    the annual changes, including one
        when volcanic ash smothered

the sun, another with astonishing floods,
    in the growth rings' micrometric widths, back
        to when, within shade, the godly Cleopatras reigned.

In hindsight, 5 AD might have been
    a better year, climatically, in the cold barn
        for the birth of Christ, and 1959 to enjoy cycling.

Now, from here on out, all I can foresee globally,
        in distant future tree rings, if they are studied,
            is that the predicted catastrophic climate hit

will have spared a dendrochronologist.

LOST SONGS

Here's a problem: the native, male
Regent honeyeater in adopting another
type of bird's song is at a real loss

to reclaim its own, and so the species
is further weakened. What female
wants to be wooed by an imposter

in a remainder forest under attack?
Attraction between speakers
of Gaelic, Sioux or Piedmontese,

should there be after-dark research,
might prove to be at its most intense
when those stressed languages are used

for the best effect. The honeyeater mimics
a parrot, clever at first, but at great length
fails to be arousing. It is a takeover

by a dominant flock of communicators –
and a loss, like Arabana and Boonwurrung,
speech and song near eucalyptuses in blossom,

back when numbers of Regent honeyeaters
were guaranteed to increase. Now,
robbed of place, they're on the edge; caged,

their recorded song is fakery played
to encourage mating far from where it once
made its thrilling invitation –

hardly, for the birds, a clear solution.

POEM

The lights are on, bright yellow
in the lemon tree, during a cold afternoon –
innumerable oval fruit
among evergreen leaves, this side
of the winter solstice;
and I am old enough to see bounty
in the tree that I planted,
the soon-to-be loaded buckets,
as a horticultural victory,
a long-distance triumph.

                              Often,
the tree looks as if it's defiantly
juggling the lemons among its branches,
umpteen dozens held at once in the air.

Now I've lost count
of those lately picked.
Yet will remember the weather,
and also see this: how limited
is anyone's capacity to give
so much away, to please.

GHOST RING

Lost things turn up
but not necessarily
for the losers of them.

When the gold ring
slipped off my left little
finger, I didn't see it.

Now, weeks later,
it's a phantom ring
below the knuckle

for me to give
a reassuring twist
but, oddly, cannot.

Worn, band and buckle –
after reluctance –
since my father died,

and earlier freed
from another stern
man's finger, his father's,

the smoothed and shiny
keeper ring's a link,
like the high-bowed ferry

crossing the bright Aegean Sea
from one historic port
to another, the greasy

anti-Covid hand sanitiser
I used on board
probably the agent

that caused the lost
connection, any number
of phone calls to the port

could not restore.
I imagine the finder
had not a thought

for the pure reward
to be had by making
such a call a good

news story, enthralled
instead by the weight
of gold, the luck,

the soon welcome
cash, no heavy loss
to be worn that day at all.

A pawnbroker in the town
where the ferry docked
said there was no call

thereabouts for the kind
of ring – ghost ring! –
I described and someone,

surely, found. A treasure
listed on the periodic table,
persistent, even if now

it's most likely melted down.
Gone, in its element, shining
like a sea the sun beats on.

DEATH, A PROSPECT

The undiscovered country –
a lot of people I know/
you know personally
have vanished there, no return
ticket, a piss off for Tripadvisor
and any travel advertisers.
Proceed with caution, I'd say
to anyone taking a rowing boat
far out into the ocean, yet
that's directly a better bet than
to consider death as a departure,
since the sea has form
although terrific storms.
There are so many lovely places
to exhaust – which cannot be said
about the subject of this short
verbal excursion; space simply
is not a problem. Death, as a gate,
makes mass tourism look quaint.
It must have caravans of fans.
But I don't plan to take
the trip just yet, which is not to say
I'm putting if off as long
as possible. I'm not. I'm not –
I still haven't been to Camelot
which may be in a nearby block –
I'll go when it's less popular.

ZEN

After all there is this –
a walk down to the shore,
and then you begin a search
for stones of a certain
size, shape and weight.
The water has paused as far out
as you can see. A gloom
has lifted (the world's woes
now are parenthetical) and
with a practiced arm action,
you skim the first spinning flat
stone across the water, watch
it leap, once, twice, oh,
next at best twenty times
at a stretch, like smoothed
stepping stones' own steps.

ABOUT THE AUTHOR

Andrew Sant was born in London in 1950. He is the author of numerous collections of poems, including three *Selected Poems*, published in Australia and the UK. He has lived in Melbourne, Hobart, and London, pursued various occupations, especially teaching – literacy to prisoners and the unemployed, English to non-English speakers and humanities subjects to students in mainstream institutions. He has also been a copywriter and manager of a hostel for juvenile offenders. Sant has travelled widely and been a writer-in-residence at several universities, including the University of Peking in Beijing, China, and Goldsmiths College, University of London. His poems have been widely anthologized and appeared in journals and newspapers such as *The Times Literary Supplement, Meanjin, The Age, Poetry Review* (UK), *Poetry* (US) *Australian Book Review*, the *Best Australian Poems* series and numerous others. He is the author of two collections of essays, *How to Proceed* (2016) and *The Hallelujah Shadow* (2020). He co-founded the long-running quarterly journal, *Island*, based in Tasmania, and remained an editor for a decade. He is a former member of the Literature Board of the Australia Council and a recipient of the Centenary Medal.

ACKNOWLEDGEMENTS

Previously published poems in this collection have appeared in *Australian Book Review*, *Meanjin*, *World Poetry*, *Falling and Flying* (edited by Judith Beveridge and Susan Ogle) and *Anthology of Australian Verse 2023* (edited by Lucas Smith).

www.ingramcontent.com/pod-product-compliance
Lightning Source LLC
Chambersburg PA
CBHW030848090426
42737CB00009B/1143